heat heat heat heat
heat heat heat heat
heat heat heat heat
heat heat heat heat
heat heat heat heat
heat heat heat heat
heat heat heat

heat

Gareth
book of quotes

Say what?
special

First published in 2002 by Contender Books
48 Margaret Street
London W1W 8SE
www.contendergroup.com

This edition published 2002
1 3 5 7 9 10 8 6 4 2

ISBN 1 84357 039 4

Edited by Julie Emery
Art Director: Mark Taylor
Picture Editor: Clara Massie
Compiled by Amy Smith
Enterprise Director for *heat*: Zachary Soreff

Pictures: Alpha; Ken Goff; Mission; Rex Features; Ross Parry Agency

Repro by Digicol Link, Kent
Printed and bound in Belgium by Proost NV

Also available:
Say what? Celebrity Sex
Say what? The Osbournes

heat

Gareth

book of quotes

Say what?
special

Home & family

"Going home to Bradford is always special. I'm proud to say I'm from Bradford and it means a lot to me that I can help raise the profile of my home town."

Mr Gates stays true to his roots...

"I'm going to buy a house up north for my family soon. They're a priority, especially because of all the fans who keep coming to the house."

...and his close-knit family

“My true idols are my mum and dad. I just wouldn’t be here now without them.”

Aaah – Gareth shows he’s a real family man

“He’s not shy really, it’s just his speech that holds him back. He told me, ‘Mum, I’ve got so much that I want to say but I just can’t say it.’”

Mum Wendy tells it like it is...

“If he ever did get airs and graces, I’d put him back in his place but I really don’t think that will happen.”

...and keeps a watchful eye on her son

“I told him, ‘If anyone offers you drugs, you get straight on the phone to me.’”

She’s not afraid to protect her boy…

“Don’t get upset and bring yourself down to their level, Mum. I am who I am and people like me whether I can speak or not.”

…while Gareth tells Wendy to ignore journalists making jokes about his stammer

"Nicola is very supportive of me. She's with me every step of the way."

No sibling rivalry between Gareth and his little sis

"He's been in the public eye for months now and he's still just a normal boy. Even when there've been cameras and reporters outside our house, he'll still walk his sister to school."

Gareth's mum Wendy on how fame hasn't gone to her son's head

"All my family are really close, my sisters and my mum and everyone, so we're always on the phone."

We wouldn't like to see the phone bills at the Gates' house

"My roots will always be in Bradford and my family are still there. But I like the idea of a bachelor pad."

He's a home-loving boy all right...

"I want the whole showbiz lifestyle, like Elvis had. The girls, the champagne, the fast cars... but I want to stay as normal as I can."

...well, maybe not *that* home-loving

“She’s great. She’s probably the person I turn to most for support.”

Gareth waxes lyrical about his mum Wendy. Bless

“I’m going to make sure my family are comfortable with a new house, car and everything. And then I’ll spend some of it on me – get an apartment, learn how to drive and get a car.”

On his plans to spend his new-found dosh

SALAD
8

Fame & fans

“I know any young man should love all that attention but when they ask me to sign their chests, I usually run away fast.”

We think you’ll get used to it

“Oooh, all the attention from the girls – it’s wicked! I love it when they run down the street after me, screaming my name.”

You may live to regret saying that, Gaz

"Last week I dressed up in a baseball cap, scarf and shades and I thought, 'Well, no one's going to recognise me in this get-up.' But they did. It's a bit weird."

Gareth fans can spot him at 20 paces, apparently

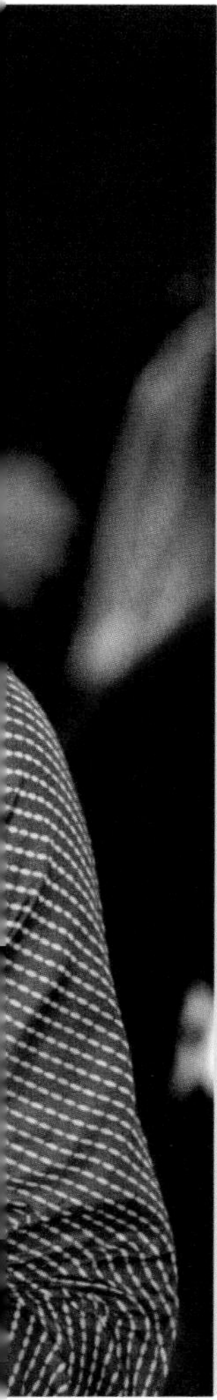

“I love the idea of being a poster on bedroom walls.”

"The important thing now is for me to keep my feet on the ground and not let all this go to my head."

You can't accuse Gareth of starry behaviour…

"I wouldn't feel happy knowing that I had all this fame, money and attention when there are people out there with nothing who are hungry, homeless and needy – I want to help those people too."

…and he really does have a heart of gold

"Someone tried to rip my shirt off once. Honestly, I was just standing there in a crowd and a girl started pulling it off me. How mad is that?"

Pretty understandable we'd say, Gareth

"I couldn't pose totally naked! No way – not for all the money in the whole wide world. I'd definitely draw the line there."

Damn! Still, he might change his mind one day. You never know

“I always want to enjoy my work, you know? I think if it gets to the point where you’re thinking, ‘Oh no, not another photoshoot,’ then you shouldn’t be doing this job.”

Gareth shows off his work ethic

“Am I the new Tom Jones? Perhaps.”

Gareth aims to be a legend

“The funniest thing is my dad was delivering them because he’s a postman and most of the letters are addressed to Gareth Gates, Bradford, Pop Idol. The sorting office gives him the letters to take home.”

Mr Gates Sr brings his work home with him

"It was great to come home to Yorkshire and all I can say is 'wow' to the sound. It almost bent my spikes back!"

On his extremely loud screaming fans at Sheffield Arena

"I get marriage proposals and I get sent loads of knickers from fans, too – in all shapes and sizes. But I don't have a preference – G-strings or bikini pants, I like them all. As long as they're not those big belly-warmer ones."

Got that, girls?

"If you have a firm belief in yourself, it's harder to drift into all the traps out there."

"I want to be as big as Elvis – but not literally, of course. And I want to see my name up in lights in Vegas."

But will he swap his white suit for a rhinestone catsuit?

"My life has changed in a huge way. I can't walk down the street without people coming up to me, but I love it."

In that case, we can't wait until we bump into Gareth on the street

“I was in a mobile phone shop and I heard these whispers: ‘It’s him! It’s him!’ and I turned round and there were four girls and they started screaming. I had to walk out of the shop, I felt too embarrassed.”

It’s him! It’s him! That pop idol who gets embarrassed!

Romance & girls

"It's very difficult for her – Hayley's had so much stick. She's had girls shouting, 'You bitch!' to her on the street. It's a real shame you can't just go out."

Gareth reveals the abuse Hayley suffered because of *those* rumours

"I want to get married one day and have loads of kids. I want a nice wife, a nice house, a nice car and a swimming pool – that would be so cool."

He wants to have it all, that Gareth

“There is a naughtier side to me, but I’m not going to show it. I’ll save that for my women.”

You know what they say – it’s always the quiet ones!

“Oooh, it just makes me melt when I smell that [Jean Paul Gaultier perfume] on a girl. Yum! I wear the men’s version too.”

The scent of a woman is very important

VOTE GARETH

VOTE GARETH

“I need a girl who is willing to understand what I’m going through and be patient with me.”

Gareth’s looking for a very special lady…

“There has been a lot of publicity about me liking her, so when I first got to sing with her I was really shy. Obviously I really enjoyed meeting her – what lad wouldn’t? Unfortunately though, she’s getting married.”

…but that lady won’t be Rachel S Club

“I love a girl who gets dressed up for an occasion.”

"I want a bird who's really classy. She has to be able to look good in jeans or a dress."

Dress to impress and you'll get Mr Gates' attention...

"At this point in my career I have to be really focused. If I had a girlfriend I wouldn't be able to spend any time with her."

...if you can drag him away from his work, that is

"I have sung to a girl before, but only once and it's too private and special to talk about."

Oh, go on, tell us!

"I'm really romantic. I like buying cute gifts for a girl, even if it's just a necklace or something."

Don't you just wish he was your boyfriend?

“When I was younger, I could never chat a girl up.”

Gareth used to be a shy boy

"I haven't got a girlfriend. If I was in a relationship with someone I'd want to spend a lot of time with them, and I haven't got that time at the moment."

He reveals how time consuming it is being an international pop star

"Although I fancy Britney, I think Shakira is hot too. Maybe I could let them fight over me."

Now *that* would be interesting to watch

Pop Idol

“Even though I didn’t actually win *Pop Idol*, I have never thought to myself, ‘I’m a loser,’ or anything.”

You’re always a winner in our eyes

“The most stressful time was waiting to find out whether you’re through to the next round or not. It was the hardest thing to cope with.”

On the weekly torture of the public vote

"A star is a star. You were fantastic. You have proved you are not a one-trick pony and you deserve all the praise you've had."

Simon Cowell quite liked Gareth's performance

"To hand over the Number One spot to Gareth was an absolute pleasure. There's absolutely no one who I'd rather it was."

Will modestly congratulates Gareth on knocking him off the top of the charts

“Hayley’s definitely a special friend.”

But exactly *how* special?

“What you have done today shows courage beyond belief.”

Simon Cowell at Gareth’s very first *Pop Idol* audition

“Gareth is the one most special to me. He has this cheeky grin.”

Awww! Zoe adores Gareth

“I didn’t know I had a voice until I auditioned for the musical *Joseph* at school.”

And we’re very glad you did

“I remember making sure I didn’t drop any marmalade and bits of toast on the application form as I filled it in. But never in a million years did I imagine I’d get this far.”

You’ve come a long way, Gareth

"My husband joined Gareth when he went filming for *Pop Idol* at a local school and when the kids saw Gareth they went mad. It was like the reaction to The Beatles."

Gareth's mum Wendy describes how crazy the local children went for her son...

"The teachers were worse than the pupils – they were pushing through to get autographs."

...but the adults were worse!

“He’s still the Will that we all know and love.”

Gareth on Will’s coming out

"We became friends in the first round of auditions and ended up in the same group. I think we get on well as we're the same age and he really makes me laugh."

Zoe speaks fondly about the pair's friendship

"Will is just absolutely wonderful. I must say that he is an absolutely awesome guy. If there's one person who deserves it, it's Will. We are really good friends."

Gareth quashes any rumours of bad feeling between him and Will

“Robbie? Oh man, as if I could take on him. He’s amazing!”

On the prospect of a chart battle with a certain Mr Williams

“Meeting Westlife was like a dream come true, it was really cool. I’ve met quite a few stars recently but for me to meet Westlife was just the biggest thing.”

Gareth talks about his adoration for Westlife

“Ali G is my favourite comedian – he cracks me up every time I see him.”

All Gareth needs is his own MeJulie

“It’s everything I always wanted. A pop star life.”

See, dreams can come true

“I am actually quite good at cooking now. Micro Chips and all that. No, I'm joking. I do a mean spaghetti bolognese.”

All back to yours for dinner then, Gareth?

"I really rate David Beckham. If Posh and Becks invited me round for tea, I'd definitely go."

So would we, Gareth

"You know, I've always admired him because he's a huge star. When I first heard I'd be going head-to-head with him in the charts I was scared. I thought, 'No way, up against George.'"

But Gareth was wrong – *Unchained Melody* beat George Michael's *Freeek!* to Number One

“When you are on a stage with 7,000 people watching you, it’s what it’s all about.”

Gareth loves performing for his screaming fans

“My gel would be the one luxury item I’d take in with me so I could make sure they [my spikes] were kept intact.”

Of course that’s what his luxury item in the *Big Brother* house would be

"I'm only 18 so there are no huge skeletons in my closet. But of course I've got other sides to me."

There's more to Gareth than meets the eye

"When I was young, I told my cousin this joke. I said, 'What do you call a man with no clothes on? Answer: rude.' Isn't that just the worst joke you've ever heard?"

Hmmm… don't give up the singing for a comedy career just yet

"Just like anyone else, I like having a laugh and getting up to mischief!"

And with that cheeky grin, we'd believe it

"He's a strong person who has put up with a lot from people – and he's funny as well."

Zoe on the private side of Mr Gates

“One thing that I will say about it is that it’s harder work than I first thought.”

Being a pop idol isn’t as easy as it looks, you know

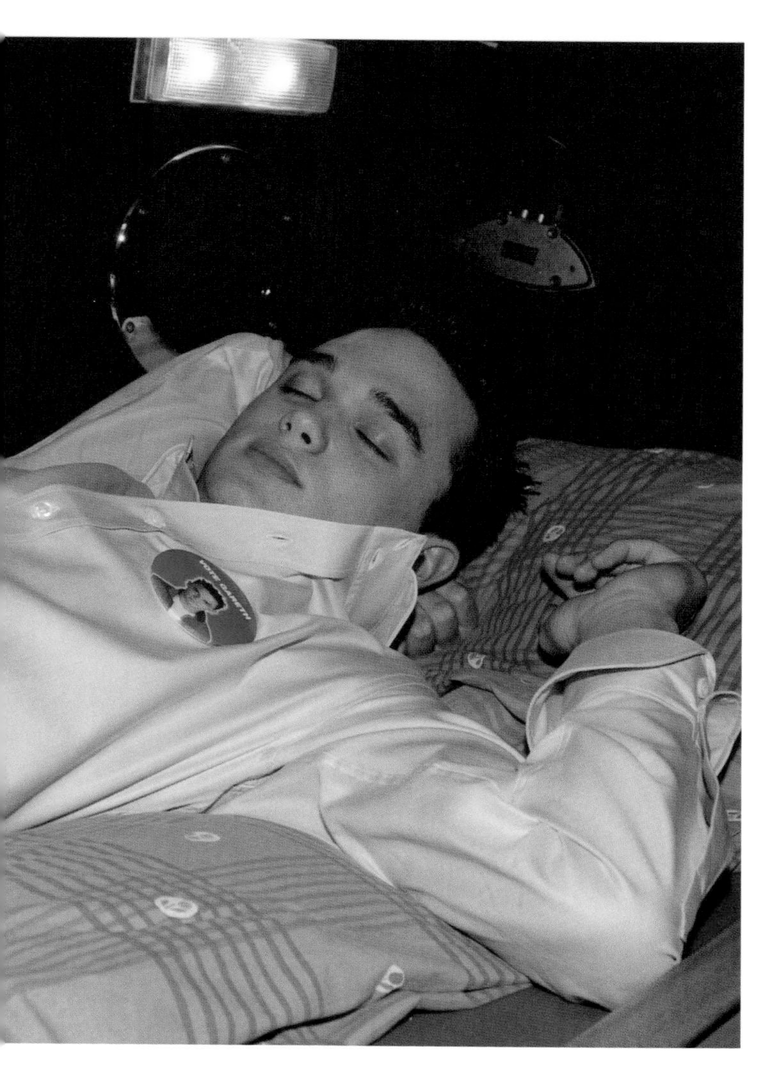

The best gossip, news, pictures, interviews, star style, horoscopes and a seven-day TV guide – every single week!

How much money will Liz get from Bing?
This week's hottest celebrity news
heat
MAGAZINE OF THE YEAR!
FIRST FOR BIG BROTHER STORIES!
Spencer!
His first magazine interview since leaving the house
On! Then off! Then...
Tom & Penélope:
"We're back together!"
They declare their love (again)
WEDDING ANNIVERSARY SOUVENIR!
POSH & BECKS:
"Our love story in pictures"
A collection of romantic photos that you just have to see!
BIG BROTHER
END OF SERIES SOUVENIR ISSUE!
with the winner
you didn't see on TV
What's worn u
ON SALE EVERY TUESDAY!